ANTARCTIC ANIMALS

by Erik Barneveld

 HOUGHTON MIFFLIN   BOSTON

PHOTOGRAPHY CREDITS: **Cover** © David Tipling/Getty Images. **1** Doug Allan/Getty Images. **2** Natphotos/Getty Images. **3** David Tipling/Getty Images. **4** © D. Fleetham/OSF/Animals Animals - Earth Scenes. **5** © D. Fleetham/OSF/Animals Animals - Earth Scenes. **6** Thomas Haider/Jupiter Images. **7** David Tipling/Getty Images. **8** Doug Allan/Getty Images. **9** Frans Lanting/Minden Pictures. **10** Steve Bloom Images/Alamy.

Printed in China

ISBN-13: 978-0-547-02955-9
ISBN-10: 0-547-02955-1

2 3 4 5 6 7 8 9 0940 15 14 13 12 11 10

Antarctica

Antarctica is a cold place.
It has a blanket of ice
that is more than a mile thick.
Many animals live in Antarctica.
These special animals can survive
in the cold climate.

Krill

Many sea animals in the Antarctic
eat krill.

Krill are tiny pink animals
that look like shrimp.

They swim in big groups
called clouds.

Big clouds of krill
can make the water look pink.

Whales

The blue whale eats tiny krill.
The whale takes a mouthful of water.
Then it squirts the water out
through a filter in its mouth.
The filter keeps the krill inside
while the water goes out.
Finally, when the water is gone,
the whale swallows the krill.

Humpback whales also eat krill.
They are famous for their singing.
Humpback whales grunt, squeak,
click, and whistle.
People call these sounds
whale songs.
You can hear these songs
from miles away.

Sperm whales do not eat krill.
They eat big fish and squid.
To find giant squid,
sperm whales dive very deep.
They go down almost two miles
and stay underwater
for almost two hours.

Penguins

The Emperor penguin is
the biggest Antarctic penguin.
It can be more than three and a half
feet tall and can weigh 65 pounds.
Its webbed feet help it swim, and
waterproof feathers keep it dry
and warm.
Otherwise, it might die
in the cold water.

Seals

Weddell seals can be
more than ten feet long.
They eat fish, squid, octopus,
and krill.
When they swim, they steer
with their flippers.
When they hunt, they dive more
than 2,000 feet and stay
underwater for more than an hour.

Leopard seals have spots
and sharp teeth.
They sometimes eat penguins.
A leopard seal might catch a
junior penguin as the
young bird is learning to swim.

Southern elephant seals spend
a lot of time in the water.
They dive deep to hunt for fish
and sea animals.
Their <mark>slippery</mark> skin helps them
move easily.
Many special animals
live in Antarctica.

Responding

Word Builder

What animals or things use steering?
Copy the chart. Write the name and how
it is steered.

Animal or thing	How it is steered
fish ?	fins and tail ?

Write About It

Text to World This story showed you some
animals that live in the Antarctic and swim
in the water. Write a few sentences about
how these animals steer when they swim.

finally	steer
junior	waterproof
otherwise	webbed
slippery	whistle

✔ TARGET STRATEGY **Infer/Predict** Use text clues to figure out important ideas.

Word Teaser Which vocabulary word means the opposite of "first of all"?